COME
PHOENIX
WORD

Published in the United States of America
by The Guild for Psychological Studies Publishing House
2230 Divisadero Street
San Francisco, California 94115

Design and Production: Dorothy Nissen
Printing: Braun-Brumfield, Inc.

Library of Congress Cataloging-in-Publication Data

Gibbons, Joan Lyon, 1924-1987
   Come phoenix word : an account of a woman's journey and struggle
for consciousness during a terminal illness : journal & writings of
Joan Lyon Gibbons, 1924-1987 / edited by Elizabeth Boyden Howes.
      p.   cm.
BR1725.G44A3   1989
248.8'6'092—dc20
[B]   89-17029
                                                              CIP

ISBN 0-917479-14-9

COME
PHOENIX
WORD

*An account
of a woman's
journey and struggle
for consciousness
during a terminal
illness*

JOURNAL & WRITINGS
OF JOAN LYON GIBBONS
1924-1987

EDITED BY ELIZABETH BOYDEN HOWES

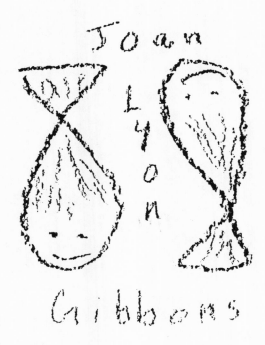

For many years Joan used this logo
as signature on papers and books.

INTRODUCTION

Die and Become—
Till thou has learned this
Thou art but a dull guest
On this dark planet. *

To be in the process of "dying and becoming" is to be with the central mythic-religious movement at the heart of things.

To be in that process when one is already, in actual fact, facing physical death is to heighten and deepen its ultimate meaning.

To *know* that one is in that process and consciously to help actualize it is perhaps the fulfillment of Selfhood and God's meaning.

Although Joan Gibbons was not healed physically after two years of acute leukemia, she did fulfill the process of psychological-spiritual transformation that she came to understand was her task.

* Johan Wolfgang von Goethe, *Selige Sehnsucht*

This small book contains excerpts from her journal of the last two years of her life, 1986-1987, which seem to express this fulfillment of consciousness while learning over and over to "die and become." Her journey was richly enhanced by a large group of people from various parts of the world, through their prayers and meditations, keeping vigil lights burning and constantly articulating love and caring by cards and messages.

Because of the way she worked and what she dealt with and achieved, it feels this book belongs not only to people who may be ill, but to all who are struggling towards this greatest fullness of consciousness.

This book, then, is not a book about Joan Gibbons, but a book about the God-Self-human dialog being actualized in the person of Joan Gibbons.

However, a few facts about her may be relevant.

She was born December 1st, 1924, in New York and she died November 13th, 1987, in Berkeley, California. She graduated from the University of California and received her Ph.D. from the Graduate Theological Union in 1979, writing her dissertation on the *Courage of Questions,* centering on the insights into the questions Jesus asked, which evidently had never been researched.

In her early married years, she was active in social and political issues, living at that time in New York, Princeton, and Washington, D.C. She was the mother of one son. She also was involved in the writing of poetry, some of which will be published later. She was a lover of words and the Word.

Later, when she moved to Berkeley, after a divorce, she became increasingly involved in the religious and psychological fields. She became an analyst in the Jungian tradition, including some study in Zurich. She travelled extensively and once gave a seminar in Jerusalem on Reconciliation.

The central focus of her interest was the Guild for Psychological Studies, where her gift of leadership expressed itself. This was especially true in the seminars on *The Records of the Life of Jesus* where her own specificity of genius flowered. She spent much time at Four Springs, Middletown, California, the center for the seminars held by the Guild.

Joan Gibbons was an urgent, introverted and passionate person. She cared about things, and nature and people, and above all, about God.

Our hope is not so much that her courage, her humor, her compassion and loveliness will show, but somehow what may come through is the Work and the How of achievement in the attempt at incarnating the meaning and specific patterning of her own uniqueness which may be a help to others.

She was guided through the late parts of her life by the words of "losing one's life to find Life." The sacrifices demanded to let the Spirit become incarnated in her substance were met prayerfully, honestly and courageously. Only thus is something approaching wholeness achieved. This journal cannot contain all of the value and content of her insights and rich relationships, especially in the last years. At the end of the book are included excerpts from journals two years (1984-1985) prior to her death, which show how intent she was, even then, to stay loyal to her dialog with God. Also included are excerpts of tapes about early life memories which she made while ill in the hospital.

Deepest thanks to all who read and helped with this book. This includes Luella Sibbald, Florence Little, John Petroni, Jerry Drino, Ann Marie Czyzewski, Donald Anders-Richards, Robert Gibbons and John Williams. And this includes the three typists, Gretchen Morgane, Janet Petroni and Lynne Gordon. But the central helper in the editing process has been Peggy Reid, whose devotion, thoroughness and thoughtfullness have helped bring this book to completion.

The acknowledgments would not be complete without a word of deep gratitude to Joan Gibbon's doctor, Martha Tracy, for her constancy of caring beyond the call of duty.

Only Silence, rather than words can express my gratitude for being with Joan Gibbons during all of her illness. The meaning of that journey for me is just starting.

Elizabeth Boyden Howes

T H E   J O U R N A L

The first entry,* *February 1986,* reads:

Word needs to rise
Like the white blood cells
rising
Anew from my bone marrow
Come Phoenix Word

* Joan Gibbons entered the hospital in January, 1986, with leukemia
and stayed until March 21, undergoing chemotherapy. During the
first month, she did not write in her journal. However, she did
record her dreams at that time. We begin this book with her first
journal entries. Following those of February, the reader will find the
January dreams.

It was felt this order would give the reader the best introduction
to her experience.

February 8—I am aware of my body
That these white cells will come
That even now the bone marrow prepares for birth
That even now the white cells prepare for birth.

February 9—Meaning
That strength come
Objectivity
The word to defend truth
Feminine approach
Substance flowers
Poetry
Once upon a time
Neatness, order, clear
Consciousness
No longer innocence
God constancy
Deeper truer love
Honesty
Reality
Practicality
Meaning

February 10—Center, Purposiveness, Meaning
Opposites included, Intensity, Passion,
Real love, Delight, Authenticity, Feminine Substance,
Spirit in Substance.
Opus—Work at consciousness—Religious passion.

February 11—Joy must be now
For life is now
Tomorrow is tomorrow

Today is now
Whatever time I live
Live now for Joy
Choose now to live.

February 16—Insight
How Spirit must serve
Substance
Harness its energies
To serve the deeper
energies of God
in matter.

Magnolia
Tuberous pink
Sun
Promise of renewal
Says "glory is"
In the midst of all darkness
"Glory is."

Mockingbird
Cry of hope
Pain of joy
Giving shadow of light.
God-presence.

Consciousness is a Work
How in this long empty day
To fill with meaning
Consciousness is choice—
I choose.

January 12—"New year"—just those two words.

DREAMS

January 18—(Four part dream)
1) *The important thing for healing is how the energy is spent.*
2) *Two young men misuse their energy.*
3) *They want to use energy for a uranium mine.*
4) *The feminine side is not conscious about use of energy.*

January 19—Sense of tremendous creativity, but couldn't quite get with it yet.

January 20—There are lots of decisions to make—two sides are hurting each other—I am not on either.

I give some appeal to both sides, but it doesn't work. I feel I will just wipe out decisions on both sides and do what is right at the moment—and be myself.

January 21—There is a beautiful brown she-goat on the hill—it will help heal me.

January 22—I became "animusy" * and a friend and I looked at one another and laughed.

January 29—A calf, I think, should be taken care of a certain way, but it hasn't been and it has died. But the next time it will be done right.

January 30—A young man gets a report about his leukemia—some things good—some bad. But it is the kind that will recur.

January 31—Wandering around a greenhouse, arranging pebbles.

* * *

* C.G. Jung defines the animus as the masculine principle in the woman, manifesting itself in positive and negative ways. Much of the time Joan uses the word in its negative connotation.

(JOURNAL RESUMES)

April 1—The swallow falls
The day is done
The world is circling
Round the sun
Let flow from the care of me
Word
Has the wind swept all away?

Down Down Down
Under the wind-swept halls
See the new beginning
Everywhere beginning

April 4—(Dreams)
1) *I write a long paper—10 pages—expressing
   Biblical meaning in my own words.*

2) *At GTU,* * the professors are expressing themselves
   with pictures—the passages include all my
   favorites—like pearl and treasure and narrow
   gate and life and destruction.*

At last a dream that shows the religious journey
moves in my unconscious. I have wondered since
coming home, if I'd ever be related to my own word.
Here I am. And in the second dream the professors
at GTU are moving to a more related place in the
unconscious. The last part affirms the primacy of
Jesus' teachings—the unconscious knows this and
gives hope for what I have come home to.

* Graduate Theological Union, Berkeley, California

April 18—I give thanks for energy returning
        for healing moving in my substance
        for sense of Being returning
        filling the empty corridors of me
I give thanks for Thou—presence
        holding these days
        in the Great Mother Thou's lap
I give thanks for love
        for increasing depth of sharing
I give thanks for all beauty of color, texture,
        light and shadow
        bird song, green in layers
I give thanks for meaning and purpose,
        to return yet with patience
        rising too from the wasteland
For all and each and more
My Thou Beloved—I give thanks.

April 25—I plan to try meditation going down to
the silent space within so better to live out of it.

May 3—God grant me now
How to live my life with meaning
Within this buttress of sickness
To do the will, live Thy glory, not give up.
But find my way.
Last night's dream of ring of gold says *Yes*
Let me now find my way
My life, whatever it is, let me live. Amen.

May 5—Strength I cry for—Objectivity
Not mealy mouth
What here for, if not able to express Word?

May 8—And now I give thanks
that "me" returns at last.
I didn't know what I was missing
Sense of possibility of life.
The energy rising of possibility
Eyes alive in mirror
No longer vacant and appealing
I give thanks
What has come
I didn't know I lacked.

May 12 & 13—Now Lord
Let courage come
One thing at a time
Let me rise to this day
Be with me.
Amen.
O God, bless me this day
Unknown, come Meaning—come
Energy for better choice—come
O Will of God
O Will of God
Come.

May 16—O God, how can I face today?
I feel I cannot endure this
agony of needle.
O God, You who want something of my life

Be present this day
O God, come into that room of needle
Help, O God, that there be
some solution to this agony
This day, O God, let truth come
Let truth come this day.
O God, O God, please—
Amen.

May 17—I give thanks, O Lord,
for yesterday—
for quiet infusion
Steady being

June 1—I see I have been treating
each new symptom as a calamity.
Must assume symptom and be
religious about it.

*June 2—(Dream) A wonderful old monk I met
in a monastery will show me illuminated manuscripts
of ancient happenings. I say of him he makes the time of
the Bible come alive.*

June 20—Home from twelve days in the hospital,
desperate at end to come home and feeling chained
by the doctor to the antibiotic needle. Anger rose to
defend me—never have I so valued freedom. And
when I cry out to a doctor, "Soul matters too," isn't
this a cry to a mechanical animus* in me—what I've
been doing to myself?

* See footnote page 17 for definition of the *animus.*

June 20—I give thanks for last night's dream.
Let my truth rise from ground levels
Then there is hope
That I can Live.

June 21—On this day when the outpouring energy
of sun finds its limits, so may I learn the limits
of mine.
O God, I will to do Thy Will
I adore Your ways
Teach me to pray
Smite me—or raise me up
I am not helpless
But move yielding to greater meanings.

June 21—Thou, this morning meditation asks You—
Do You know You tried three times to kill me?
Pneumonia at birth, cancer and leukemia?
Do You really know this! Is it intentional?
Is Your hand toward me still?
Who am I before You! Stop!
I am here. One dot in Your evolutionary sweep—
I am trying to face truth more, am
learning from this darkness.
But O Thou, I am learning and
I pray for Life—time in which to Be.
I know these days are—and why
should I ask to count on life in
more than days, still I do.

June 24—For this day,
O Thou, for this day

I pray healing, soul and body.
You have smitten me.
How can I pray, "smite me or heal?"
I do, and praying so, ask,
God be conscious.
May each hand know the other's action
Why did all this have to happen?
Surely I am more conscious
Released from certain specific responsibility
Released to—truth, honesty, courage
Released to—love-opened being
Released from negative animus
Released to feminine and Self
to enter into a pine cone
and "put out my finger and find Thee."
Thank You and Amen.
I give thanks for this day, for its energy and peace.
May I keep with the feminine more
Now and in the evening to come.

June 25—My Thou Beloved,
Smite me or heal me.
What is needed for this journey?
This day I will stay with the healing
feminine against all pull to animus.
O Thou, I will have the courage to
Do Thy Will.

June 26—Having struggled with gas
much of the night
I now know "sufficient unto each day
is the evil and grace thereof."

July 3—Having just read Mark Pelgrin's *And a Time to Die,** I am awed, sobered by the similar facets of our situation, whatever their cause. He helps me to stay with the Now, to accept that "who I am" has meaning, and stop apologizing for "who I am not."

July 6—Reading in the *Choice is Always Ours*** on trusting the healing process of the unconscious—that there is the Other with Wisdom deeper than the ego's, that this Other also is God. I must learn to let go—to trust—to work with this Process of the Other, which has most recently come in sickness!

July 7—God, may I focus on You,
There is a mystery beyond me I sense.
I am obedient to You, O God
"Over again I put out my finger and find Thee."
My focus is on Your Mystery
And I go looking beyond ephemeral facts
To the eternal fact of You.

God, I go sobered
But not afraid.

(Dream) I am in a biology group led by a woman, and she can tell that I see something, for she asks me and I tell her of slug-fish in swampy place. She is

---

* A vivid account of a man dealing religiously with terminal cancer.
** An anthology on the religious way, edited by Dorothy Phillips, Lucille Nixon, and Elizabeth Howes. Published by Harper & Row and available from Guild for Psychological Studies Publishing House.

excited and says we will gather the group together and
study them. I wonder if I am well enough to begin
research.

July 8—All right now, where are You?
Hidden, manifesting Yourself
in symptoms, sorrow, cries.
We are here
So gladly here
Bouncing on the boulders of Yourself;
You bring us drive in Your seeing.
Here, here we are
Breathing, laughing,
Dying in darkness
But alive in our dying.

Four fish darting in the hidden pool
Slow crayfish crawl around the border
Frog leap, cry, and ogling eye
For peace between us
All the ways of bearing, helping
All mysteries of Thou
Moonstones in place
For each, Halleluia.

July 9—Why shouldn't God, whom I can perceive
everywhere around me be also within me!
Why is that so hard to know?
Is God excluded from me, but everywhere else?
O Thou, O God majesty and molecule,
creator and destroyer,
I feel the dignity of You in me

in the objective presence of You
I hold up my head.
My worth is because of You
For You am I brave
For You I fight for Truth
To give You home
I open my feminine grace to Your presence.

July 11—To feel joy
To know that moment of peace continues
Deer wander up through the meadow
Birds swoop and dive among blackberries.
Everywhere peace
And inside, an end to pain
Healing, healing of the organs comes
And time feels eternal.
I am not deceived.
I know at any moment darkness strikes.

But I walk in all the healing process I know
And I give thanks for every "tidge" of beauty
For one alive leaf in my plant
My survival comes now
For each and every step of healing.

July 12—Peace
Underwater undulations of green
Among gold dart of fish
In the heart time
Eternal without clock
Guard
Alien to emergent world

How hold still in evolution
Hold moments, being
Until of own being, more
Eternal time moves a rhythm
Splendiferous rainbow
Through the world of time.

July 13—Mystery of dark
Dishonor, cheating, low
Mystery of wrong, the ugly choices
Mystery of sliding through the portals
Undisturbed
Mystery of ignoble
Underneath the noble face
Mystery, beloved opposite
Dark necessity behind the pure
Mystery of wholeness
And the wisdom born.

*(Dream) I wake up with sense of poison in my mouth
that I must not swallow.*
This is a recurrent dream, of something poisonous
that if I actually ingested it, it would kill me. What is
the poisonous attitude? It is a combination of
negative and feminine attitudes from childhood,
keeping me in unconsciousness—but finally is
overcome in battle with symbol of consciousness.

July 14—The deepest healing dilemma
I confront is now not to be
devastated by criticism.

How to include my own imperfection
And not be devastated by seeing it.
Now—what will I do—enlarge
The tent of myself—include the
superficial, noisy, fussy, nibble, unthinking,
cold, insensitive, unfeeling?
Like the fool, can I laugh? There you are!
I simply can't have it devastating to be imperfect.
This peace I long for now is not
true healing in its avoidance of stress.
I can't prepare for devastation
I can prepare for inclusion of imperfection
And that is healing.

July 15—O God—I'd like to spend today
Just breathing You in and out
So "dwell in the presence of the Most High."
That all else is in perspective.
I don't have to go to "Christ in the Desert"*
to find You. "Over again I put
out my finger and find You."
Thou, everywhere best, emergent
Best in the world and in me
Help me to include Your opposite of darkness
So I am not surprised by it
So I can work with, through it, to Your best.
Thou, come—in Thy bliss—in every cell
In coming, bless my cells with Your presence,
And be Yourself blessed in this welcoming Substance.
Day is the moment of God-presence.

* Monastery in Abiqui, New Mexico, which Joan loved.

There is nothing else.
Who knows what happens tomorrow?
So postpone nothing of consciousness.
The word of love, of affirmation is now—
God bless this now.

July 16—Do You feel the aliveness of us?
I see You—feel You—love You
Then stay, never go again
Grant us Substance
We are ridiculous, today—turning
The world You know upside down
Laughter we are
Delight in beauty
Depths we are

Sower in the meaning of things to come—
I am here. Thank You.

July 17—Come Feminine
Come Meaning
Dreams bring such warning
of energy misuse
I have not enough called God.
O Thou, larger than sickness and healing.
O Thou, larger than feminine and masculine
Come with Your reality of *best*
There is a *best* I can live
in these days of suspension of all but healing.
O God, I pray for myself
that leukemia not return,
that pneumonic hole fill in with lungs,

that kidney becomes normal,
that liver becomes normal
that the healing of substance
take place in my body.
O God, I pray for myself.

July 18—I wait each day not knowing
where darkness will strike.
And appreciate moments of peace,
calling them darkness.
I suffer that my plant has died.
But I don't confront the dying of myself.
What are the deaths? Not death-rebirth—
Death, where I permit power to others
and nothing comes to my defense.

July 22—I give thanks for last night's dream of Wise
Old Woman and Healer who must come together—
Let me feel them both as powers within me.
The healing coming from the lesser side—
not lesser but less privileged, advanced.
You who know the healing of hardship,
You who know the wisdom of suffering,
Feminine and masculine gifts.

July 23—This morning I heard the difference
between touching the Self (I have) and
living from the Self (not enough).
I see I need to bring into manifestation
that which I touch.
For vertical meditation I took my begonia—
so beautiful in life—so almost dead—with one leaf

alive. Will it move to transformation? I don't know,
but it is a Self symbol of opposites, life and death and
transformation to Third Point.

July 24—Now in the flow of this day may I stay
with barnyard, keep together Wise Old Woman
and Healer, let boy meet girl by riverbank,
heal the carp
and protect the baby birds
This day—all you helpers—come.

July 25—How can I "live from the Self"?
Remember where I have been touched,
Been gripped by a symbol of the Self
On Sicily, Pan surrounded by adoring beasts
I felt I'd never leave.
At Montserrat, high on those steps
The bird soars across the valley to a further peak
Eternity touched there.
In the Vatican, the child riding the mermaid
"Stop, come back," they cried.
These scenes are in me—I know
what is behind them is mine.
Now to touch that and live the *best*
in outer choices.

July 26—"O frabjous day!
Callooh! Callay!
he chortled in his joy." *
So say I on seeing three new leaves on my begonia.

* From *Through the Looking Glass,* Lewis Carroll.

I have saved it—it is saved. Life wins in this small
arena—not won yet—is winning
I saw one leaf
and trusted water and care, water and care
and mystery and will to life
would do the rest. I give thanks. I give thanks.

July 30—And what is death,
O brothers of the rainbow
And what is death,
O sisters of the year?

July 31—At last night's banquet at Four Springs
I got "Robbers" and "Heal,"
which spoke not of healing robbers,
but how robbers are part of the healing process,
bringing the original wound without
which one would not gain the benefit of healing.
So I spoke of loving the robbers.
I'm not sure I'm there in feeling,
but I do affirm the meaning,
That Thee in me be strengthened in presence
That the feminine in me become a way of life
That the masculine in me serve you both
Now—Now starting this day. Amen.

August 10—I wish I understood why hearing lists
of people and their problems exhausts me. For so
long a numbness protected me—as though my own
disaster was so great I was immune to others. Now
in this healing time, the disasters of others flow
into me. I hear the wound, the cry beneath. This is

something new I must protect, not run from but
slowly work with.

August 12—But what is healing?
Not to ask forgiveness for something not done.
What is healing?
My body is now much better.
Energy returns slowly.
Healing is to face darkness
where ever it comes.
Sickness is darkness in my guts.
And yet learn, from Keats, be vulnerable.
Trust the Holy Spirit
Not run from darkness.

August 24—Slowly sense of wisdom
of eyes open wide, of peace upon
my face, relaxed.
I can speak with authority,
For authority is no longer Spirit
but Spirit/Substance
Spirit pulls—substance pulls—
Birth pulls. I give thanks.
As though I might now be well
For the first time in my life.

August 25—And yet I must still ask
Why so wounded by glance of upset?
Suddenly "Off to the garbage dump.
You must be like Barbie,* perfect."

---

* Barbie was a sister, killed in an accident before Joan's birth.

Now in that very moment can I say,
"I'm not Barbie"? I must say it constantly,
every day. "I'm not Barbie, I don't have to be
perfect. I can annoy, upset, bug people. The wound
in the rainbow is O.K."

August 27—In *Green Pastures,* * the line that most
stays with me is, "I know you ain't talking to me. Is
you talking to me?" Hits my need to be sure God
knows I'm talking to Her/Him.

    A week from today, home to Berkeley and
seeing doctor. How I dread that! Not that I expect
something wrong, but in the great unknown, who
knows? I must stay gently in the healing
process, caring for trees, gathering
bottles, relating to people. God bless this
day and the consciousness thereof.

August 28—Sense of betrayal by reality, receipt of tax
problem. Felt I wasn't understood. Need to give to
myself, "O my dear, you hurt." Feel that which was
going to protect me will not. What savior did I yearn
for? Is this further healing?

August 29—The time has come to stop doubting
myself, to stop assuming guilt, to take authority of
what I know: I am not Barbie. I am not Joan, finally
to be Barbie. I am Joan who has been very sick, who
needs to defend herself, who doesn't dwell in a

---

* Drama written by Mark Connelly, first performed in New York,
   1930.

placating, nervous system. Could I examine the
synopsis of the past and simply say,
"These are no longer true?"

September 11—Come, Holy Spirit
Come with particular yearning
Into my specific substance
You are virginal, newborn
of mystery, quivering with birth.
Into my moment come
O beloved,
You are my beloved Grace
Hope, possibility
For Your coming is my world transformed.

Now in the days ahead, what shall I do?
Help with Suffering Servant.
Help with Holy Spirit, coming virginally.

September 13—(Four Springs)
This last morning I sit in the living room with Verdi's
Four Sacred Pieces. Sunrise at Standing Stones. At
peace in the beauty. Amazed to be alive. Standing
ovation at the banquet—hip hip hooray.

    It is as though in sickness I laid everything
down and now can choose to be and do. Can I? I
can and need to. I must not drive myself with coffee.
Relationships are purer, as though something
contaminated them before. I see the sickness gained
honor and authority for me. I am awed at what has
happened. The homecoming can be an integrative
time.

September 20—My insight today is the recurring
emptiness. I can't call this the result of chemotherapy. I knew it in childhood. I had hoped out of
the long sickness to be transformed. But is not so. I
am still too dependent on patterns outside myself.

September 22— (Carmel) If you were to go down,
and down and down, what would you find? Is there
a jewel? One single love-filled jewel waiting to be
gathered, to the surface of being.

      Look, gather in right now
You cannot continue empty
You were not born for that
You did not live for that
O God, O Self in my deeps
I cannot live without You
O Holy Spirit, You which are
Into the particularity of my substance,
Come.

September 23—Beautiful dream. Let me learn to
relax. Out of relaxation comes initiative, the virginal
open to the Holy Spirit.
      Beautiful morning on beach—
waves curling,
translucent, never want to leave.
What's alive in me now?
Peace. Feminine. Real challenge to be feminine
at home. I run to animus when I am alone and it
leaves me empty.

September 24—(Dream) There are two books I want
very much to buy. One is about a little blonde girl with
a dutch boy cut and how she took the initiative. The
other is on how to relax all over one's body. At a
central point is the relaxation. A bell rang in a church
tower that helps the person know that what was being
done was right. I go to a monastery to see if they will
sponsor my study and give me $5 cash to buy the two
books. The woman I talk to is not impressed with the
second book because of the ringing of the bell. She says
such an experience should be inner and not dependent
on an outer event. I am disappointed but feel I can go
elsewhere for the books, for this will be my life work,
to relax and help others to do so. The introduction
to relaxing had come while visiting the monastery.
I had been lying down with a cover over me while the
monks did their thing. A woman comes along and tells
me a better way to relax and she starts to teach me how
and S. comes and helps. I begin to dance, freely,
gracefully, joyfully. At first I resist and then I decide to
buy the book and really learn.

September 24—(Dialog with the Other)
Referring to a dream of a woman dying:

I: The dying woman troubles me. Why is
            one dying just at this time I am trying to
            be in touch with the Feminine? She
            knows where she wants to be and what
            she wants to have.

The Other: You, who are dying, why is it? Can't
something be done?

I: My spirit is just going. I feel life forces
ebb. Medical reports are discouraging.

The Other: You have let go to despair.
That's not the answer.

I: What alternative is there? There is really
no hope, and you deceive yourself in
"feeling better."

The Other: Look, we're up against a mystery.
We just don't know what's coming next,
if anything.

I: My doctor has fears, expectations of
something going wrong. She speaks from
experience. And the chart showed kid-
neys, liver, red blood, platelets all not
healed.

The Other: And yet there is more than the medical.
That is what we are about now,
in meditation, in poetry, writing,
dialoging with God. There is more, but
that's not enough. Look, right now you
are surrounded by feminine love, your
three friends who can sustain life, real
feminine life. You haven't done too well.

I: No, but I am trying to change
and I need You.

The Other: How can I help?
By not despairing with death. Come take

hold of life with me. Emerge from your
heaviness.

I: I will come, but you must help me.
I will.

(Carmel)
The beautiful simplicity here evokes the feminine,
need to bring this home, clear-eyed, with dignity and
courage and authority, so I can live full energy in the
present and future. This must be a future for now.
Holy Spirit, come with the particularity of this
moment.

September 25—Still keeping dignity, presence, love
of substance here at home. Brought sand home. As
stood by the edge of the sea, I prayed for meaning,
joy, peace, strength and healing. How can I hold
them here in this house and not be lost?

    I am sensitive, shy, friendly, loving, wide-eyed,
intelligent, humorous, generous, thoughtful,
feminine and loved.

September 27—I am I
of feelings, intensities
Love of a leaf, golden against a pine.
I am I
I have a heart
There are meanings, pain
Memories, regrets.
But present time, O now, right now to be lived.
Look, look, look

Feel, remember beauty
I am I, now living, now loved
I am I.

September 29—Saw doctor today. Learned that
leukemia cells have been "in sanctuary"*
could come out at any time.
It awakens me to reality
What do I want to do, with time left?

October 4—(At Four Springs)
Now here again
O poetry of soul
Healing place
Look, my legs with energy climb
My consciousness is vibrant
My eyes gleam
God, I give you thanks—this healing
ounce by ounce—I am returned to myself
Come now, feminine of Carmel
Come now, spirit of Four Springs
Come now new child of Being—Now.

October 5—O, how shall I keep cells "in sanctuary"*
if some there be?
O, how shall I not be vulnerable
again to cancer?
I no longer seek exit.
I want life now.

---

* "In sanctuary": This refers to leukemia cells that reside in organs
 chemotherapy reaches poorly or not at all, such as the central nervous system.

Life rises and wants to Be.
New tendrils come.
What is that which kills?
Word. Word. Word. Word where are you?
God Word rooted in Being.
Where are you?
Thou, what is forgiveness?
Thou, what is healing?
Go to the Source, the very Source.
Find the life which is your own.

October 6—A healing time
Slow Slow Slow Slow
A year ago, a year ago
I was dying and didn't know it.

October 8—O, the consciousness
Cry for consciousness still needed.
Who died? Who needed to die but didn't?
Mealy-mouthed is still alive
Always to haunt me
And that is the drama within me.
Not I, but see, see
with consciousness. Be objective. Not identify,
courage now. This is your soul's battle. Be objective.
See, I am not mealy-mouthed!

October 11—*(After reading Van der Post's*
The Lost World of the Kalahari*)*
O child of a Bushman.
You, you
In my dream impregnating me

Mystery, Mystery
What child shall be born of us?
Is there some authentic word
Born out of unconscious mystery
And the mystery of the conscious I?
O, are you the Source I seek?
Something strong enough to encompass
opposites and not be overwhelmed?

October 12—At last night's party I danced to the
music of *Zorba* as though the last time—or first—and
this morning thought of my birthday party to come.

October 13—O you child of a Bushman, you!
How my heart rings with this.
When I was a child, what would it have been
if someone had given me her?
This day a creative leap in me.
O Bushman.
Heart moving behind my heart,
Take me now to the depth behind all places,
To the place eternal, unplanned, of birth.

October 14—More clearly let me learn
what can and cannot be fed into my insides.
I so love chocolate—but not good inside
combined with tension. Surely I have
evolved to will and sense a higher value.

See, see the great bird
Wise, twinkling eye

Refuse the tempting fruit
Turn from gleaming succulence

See, wise head turn
Wings beat the ear and rise
Elsewhere to go
Elsewhere to go
So you
So you also can.

October 15—Bird of Wisdom
Others saw you in me
I, only in others
O Bird, O Bird let us be together
In the quiet now
In the quiet now
Cry Cry Cry Cry
Bird cry in your soul
Wanting to be
Cry Cry in your world
You can still be.

October 18—Banquet words: "Resist not"
"No/Yes Brothers"*
So face the No still dark.
O Bird, guide to consciousness.

October 19—O dream that is dreaming me
A myth of my own reality

* Refers to Jesus' parable, *Matthew 21:28-31*

What shall I choose this day?
Let's pick vegetables
Let my myth come from my own deeps
O be honest, honest. What do I want this day?
Order, more notebooks in order, that's for future.
What for present? Deep breathing.
This how not get caught in darkness.

October 20—O Bird of Wisdom, tell me,
Out of where in my heart comes mercy, gratitude?
See the bird come upon to harvest of berries,
saved from winter's storm.
Sing before eating
Send into the unknown, choirs of song, gladness,
Gratitude, a harvest of notes for that other mystery.
So life now
So Life now is that sudden feast.

October 21—O tapping, tapping, tapping of my spirit,
What shall I do?

Listen, listen, listen to the invisible
Heart throb within you
With every beat, life that is not you, affirms itself.
Listen
Being is, caged in the web of civilization.
Listen in the midnight born of your soul
Life is!
Let go. Do what must be done within the webbings.
Live, with the sure silent beat of your own heart
beating.
Keep your focus there.

October 24—O so many mystery blossoms
This day I am sick with something.
Must go somewhere for help.
Why not enough learned?

October 25—And discovered shingles.
Why? "Pain is the most beautiful of the colors
of becoming," so says Mantis.*
Now, for how many months I must live with pain?
Listen to, move around and with.
O God, gratitude that no more.
Help me to endure this much, and
not get worse, and not have to take medicine.

*October 26—(Dialog with Bushman from dream
not recorded):*
O this is a mysterious gift of a dream.
Bushman, I am here.
         Thank you for returning.
I am almost beyond words. How can I not lose you?
Stay close to mystery. Trust that collected words
have meaning. Trust the subterranean working in
you all your days. The almost lost, the almost lost
remains there still in the poetry. The "once-upon-a-
time" remains. All is well.

October 27—Pain is intense today.
O Thou, God of creation
Help now to objectivity
Beyond pain there is Thee

---

* A figure in African myth. See *Patterns of Renewal* by Laurens Van
   der Post, Pendle Hill Pamphlet.

Within pain there is Thee.
O God, how be objective?
Thou, thank you for Your coming.
Your presence makes a difference.
I must come out of this place of pain
No matter how much it hurts.
I must stay outside it.

October 28—Was hysterical yesterday with pain.
Said I wasn't sure I'd have the needed courage.
Then know I must.
Just that. I must have courage.
Do what must be done.
Survive the pain
Live as best as I can
So I give thanks to God
Who says: you must.

October 30—Awoke grateful for less pain, for last night's release in guts. And for response to my cry of yesterday afternoon to a Thou beyond, who had created the world and cared for me and a Thou within, who knew Shabat was happening in my inner world.

So please God, may I learn before You have to do more. May I learn Your Will for me. I give thanks. Amen.

October 30—O God, Mysterious Thou, let me learn when to move, when to stay still. When I feel better, O Thou, let me stay still in a place of healing gentleness. God, You are present. I give thanks.

October 31—O God, upon this Halloween night I
cry out to You, I give thanks for Your merciful
healing and lessened pain. O Thou, I do pledge to
learn to be more still, and yet in courage confront
those moments of "you must."
I pledge to learn and I give thanks. Amen.

Thou art in my body now
Talking with me
Be ever with me
Moving Your healing presence
Through all my bone marrow,
all my nerves, all my guts.
You know where You are needed
You go there swiftly and I give thanks. Amen.

November 1—O God, I so prayed to animus
this morning. Ran my obedient, kow-towing path,
unheard, unnoticed. So whom had I served? What
he? "Tyrant in my deeps."

O Bird, stay with feminine
Only deep balance of feminine
Is resilient enough not to react to animus
Deep feminine laughs
Deep feminine sees
And when She moves
She moves with strength.
God says to do His Will.
I must wait and listen
before I act.

November 2—I will take time to discern Thy Will
I pray for steady ears
I pray for steady heart
And now to day's end, O Thou,
Thank you for Holy Spirit presence
reminding in that very hour how to be.
I pray for healing for broken blisters,
Healing most for broken soul.

November 3—Learned this morning to call on
Locust and her pots.* Otherwise animus rises so
quickly. Today, a year ago, I must have been so sick.
Today 62 years ago I was moving toward birth. I
wonder what toxics were already in my body. I am
living much more now moment to moment, with
much gratitude for every beauty given.

November 4—God, this is a great mystery
I give Thee thanks for what I've learned:
Something about pain—and strength,
Something about immune system—and vulnerability,
Something about reality,
Animus and locust.
I thought of how I was conceived,
from one sperm, one ovum
Out of my father's body, out of my mother's body,
Out of regenerative cells each inherited.
What complacency to forget such a beginning.
So I pray now to Thee, creating cells,
Enter each cell of my body.
No more leukemia, no more disease.

* Refers to Navajo Coyote Myth.

Let what is left of my life be lived with meaning.
Amen.

November 5—A pink blossom coming
on my resurrected plant!
I was dead and now that you have come
I live again. Halleluia!
Thank You, God presence.

This day I give thanks for political wisdom of my
land to return a Democratic Senate. And for myself,
thanks for new perspective.

November 6—I again commit myself to eat wisely.
God help me—this is Your body!
O God, we must find our places for joys.
Deeper joys that don't just tittilate taste buds and
destroy within, but joys that delight on all levels.

November 7—O God, I feel distracted.
Is it only peril that throws me to Thee?
Must be more or else peril everywhere.
O God, Thou art within me, cell for cell.

November 8—(*On this day she went home from
Four Springs*)

November 9—How be objective, coming home?
O Thou, I give thanks.
Home is good to come home to, shingles better.
O Thou, I commit my will to Thine.
I've been so unconscious.
Am I still so? I do know more.

But now go slowly, in all wisdom.
Such joy this day—see all things
for the first time and love them.

November 10—Each day I must choose
the numinous:
Music this morning
Meditation on Thee
Time for soul, time to write
Bushman-bird myth.
O Thou, I will my will to do Your Will.
Help me. Amen.

November 11—Thou, I have forgotten Thee.
I must learn what happens
when compulsions get me.
O Thou, keep me with You.
Remember Yourself in me
Otherwise someone else lives my life.
Bless Myriam. Bless Wendy's parents.
O mystery of darkness, bless Thee.

November 12—Let it be a day of soul,
Granted now life, and time to choose
Granted now release from pressure.
Let pressures not come from within.
What are the symbols of my soul?
The feathers, sand and shells, violets,
birthed plans, garden, mending, bells, Thy Will.
Honor these this day
And bless this day, Myriam and Wendy's parents.

November 13—O Thou, watch over me.
I pray an end to these shooting pains.
And if this cannot end now, I pray
better to endure them. I keep sensing your intent,
that I stay slow.
Thank you bird song now in my dark garden.
Let me learn to feast upon the everywhere,
symbol of Thee.

November 14—O God, having just failed You, I see
that every single choice must serve You, or negative
animus rules. Forgive me.

November 15—What can I learn about enduring
great pain? "It will pass" is solace. Suppose it does
not pass? Slowly can I emerge and not be possessed?
God, with me, that's our task. "Shape up or ship
out." Do you agree with it? To some extent. It's no
good worrying about pain. When it is going to
come, how prevent it. Be wise. See if it can come not
in push and drive, but just in courage. I can see I
have gone down under again. Feel beaten by this
new onslaught. And there are the troops, those that
need me. So courage and strength.

November 18—O Thou, what is Thy Will?
What do people do with this pain?
Be patient with it. Bring love to it.
Not thrust it on an enemy.
Love Suffering Substance. Yes.

November 21 —Thou, I give thanks for lessened
pain, for graciousness last evening. Let the healing
involved in this birthday be a deep one, of the fun I
always wanted, of the joy I always wanted. Foolish
loving as part of the mystery in life.

In the midst of all dark things let there be—
Rivendell, Tom Bombadill*—a place of honor and
beauty. Glory Glory Glory Glory.

November 22—These days move slowly. Am I
learning enough from pain? How can I learn not be
active when symptoms are no longer there? Is this a
statement of the power of my compulsive animus and
weakness of my ego, however committed to Thee? I
seem not to resist enough the pull of good collective
patterns. That takes consciousness. My tendency is to
enjoy flow, but flow flows into animus. Each choice
must have Your Will at the center.

What good to pray for consciousness if I don't
live it enough? I must not weep. I live too much in
my own world. I guess I'm running from last year's
despair. I felt hopeless then. Now I have changed.
Am going more slowly. But the crux, the point of
going is the same—no more running away from
unconsciousness.

November 23—I think of the supreme moment of
truth last year at this time when my nephew was told

---

* Rivendell and Tom Bombadill's home were both havens in Tolkien's
Lord of the Rings.

by his young wife that he was dying of cancer. Let
me learn courage and honest love from this and how
to deal with my son with more courage and honest
love.

November 24—Thou, I will be glad when this pain-
itch is over. Now I am silent and quiet more of the
time. The energy that rises does not have to act. This
day let me prepare my home for my birthday party
—room by room—beautify and nesting. One gift at
last, not only to see what needs doing, but to act on
it. I know healing for me includes strengthening and
objectivity. What will make me so? *"You* must know
you're not a mouse!"

November 26—Today let me see truth.
There is much to do today.
Let me do the needed simply.
Let me keep to the essence.
Let my own desire and initiative grow,
Not animus, but feminine.

At last I understand.
Death is only death
But a living death is worse.

November 27—Happy Thanksgiving.
God, I give thanks for life and pledge to live it better.
This day let me stay objective and strong. Let that be
Thanksgiving—present to us—that laughter come
instead of subjectivity. Now let objectivity come!

November 28—It is so hard to be wise!
Thou, grant me not to get sick.
O Thou, I don't want to be put down again.
If I had life, how would I live?
Choose. Could I choose a bit more? Choose life.
O Thou, I do choose life, let me have the chance.

November 29—Time will be gone and I will not have
said goodbye to 61. *(Her birthday–December 1)*
A year of pain
Agony of Substance
Curbing of Spirit
To year of purpose.
Welcome to 62.
O eye, eye in this new year,
Come. Beyond me yet come
That I do Thy Will.
Yet know I am blocked from within.
What do I lack? Courage? Will?
Awe? Commitment? Love? Imagination?
Meaning? Reverence? Mystery? Preparation?
Objectivity?
O Thou, Creator of all beautiful patterns, I will
serve creative pattern. Amen and thank You.

November 30—To give this party feels right.
May it be creative, fun and not animusy.
May the fun place in me that wants this
kind of party be blessed.

May I now become new and be granted wholeness as achievement of the rest of my life. I said I

would accept my destiny, whatever it might be, and
not run away from it. So let it be.

December 1—Happy Birthday, Joan, to me—
I am 62. Such a tender party. Moments I wanted
never to end.

And their last tender singing of *Happy Birthday*.
I had the sense of it being my last birthday.

I give You thanks, O Thou—
You were celebrated.
When my son said he was glad I was giving to myself
rather than to him, I understood how I had given to
myself through him.

December 2—You can learn from mistakes.
Yesterday did too much. Did lovely things
but wasn't present enough.

Despite itch of shingles, I feel better than
anytime since sickness. Energy and vitality—that is
good. Lesson of 62—go slow—do not rush into
activity.

Giving arise in my heart but be sure
to give to myself
Joy and honor and love
Stay with them.
O Thou, is this Thy birthday gift to me?
I give thanks.

December 3—Thanks for all the healing process.
May I learn!
O Bird help me

Go step by step
Not raucous
See, as the hawk rides the wind
Ride the wind of truth
Learn the currents
Ride the wind of your own being.

December 4—O Bird of Truth,
There is one song, one sky
Two wings to fly.
One wrong
To fly as though you're going to die
To fly too high.
Belong not with the throng
But fly along
And then you will not lie.

I broke in with my mind and so gained the end.
Truth in poetry is to be authentic to what rises.
This must be a day of honoring truth.

December 7—*(Four Springs)*
And it came to me last night I must give
more love. My heart moved in response.
O Soul, blossom this day—blossom with
love, with Feminine.

December 8—This day go with Love, including
love of myself. This blooming plant fulfills
my soul, an eye-feast. These Advent candles fulfill
delight. The long view to hills fulfills mystery.
O God for this Your Presence, I give thanks.

December 10—O Self, larger than pain,
I will serve Thee.
What will find me in the creche?
No more Herod or innkeeper—a sheep perhaps.
Your obedient servant.
The camel who bends his head to see the Child.
O Child, I pray for everyone else.
I pray now you be born in me.

December 11—Wound of this seminar is not leading.
What has happened to my creativity?
Step by step will it emerge?
Aware in seminar session I bring authority of insight.

December 12—Spirit in the limitation of substance.
I love and have loved so long.
May I bring love and tenderness
O, "Christ in the desert"* be blessed.
Someday I return to you—in the hallows.

December 15—Thank You for Covenant in the
creche we made. The rainbow I made is between us,
O Thou. Thank You for that affirmation of what we
have.

December 16—O Thou, let Thy Covenant
be with me in consciousness.
Patience, obedience, commitment, courage—
these are my gifts to the Child.
I am experiencing more dullness of late—

* See footnote, page 28.

with moments of vitality.
Is this what dying feels like?
The slow battening down of the hatches?

December 18—Last day of '86 at Four Springs.
Elizabeth's toast to me at banquet "You will always
be first 'inheritor'" moved me to tears.
Bless seminar over—I have to grow, like Lazarus
returned from dead. I am heard and honored.
May I go home and enjoy Christmas and Palm
Springs. Give what I can, not too much.
Honor Thee and the growing depths between us.

December 19—Now with gratitude for home
welcoming me—for all its tangibles of love,
everywhere warmth-care. May I cherish this home
and its substance. Now a cough. I am depressed.
Let go. Let go. Let go. Let go.

December 20—So I do have a cold. Hold me, that
this not worsen. Remember Your Covenant.
Remember Your Rainbow.

December 21—O God, I pray,
Where are You in my deep?
I am here. Stay close to me today.
I am in your substance
In every cell of you.
In sickness and in healing.

December 22—God, have mercy
Christ, have mercy
I cannot live today unless I am conscious.
How shall I express love?
Limited. Housebound with cold.
O God of loving, giving generosity
Dwell in my heart
Manifest in my attitude
Let me be warm
Live in me this day, objective Love.

December 24—Merry Christmas-Eve Day.
This day may I be sensitive and bring love
Yes, the bounty of Santa Claus.
What is he? The one with enough love and
tangible gifts for everyone, who comes mysteriously
and answers all longings. A kind of Self-forgiveness
which is why he comes on day the Child is born.
He comes down chimney, wears red, not exclusive—
can enter every home through chimney! Comes on
sled, pulled by reindeer, helped by elves. Merry
Christmas.

December 25—Merry Christmas—as if this were
my last. Let there be light.Thank you. This is the day
of celebration of the birth within and in the world.
Let each gift given and opened be a celebration of
qualities of the Child. The day also celebrates the
birth of Jesus of Nazareth—amazing man.
Bless this day. Bless the whole world.

December 26—Learn while you still can.
Yesterday, too much giving without mature meeting.
Gifts sensitive, but too much.

December 27—Tomorrow to Palm Springs—
May we be blessed.
May the New Year come with health
May I honor Substance
May I also honor Spirit
Unless both are, Something dies—
Let the light of consciousness remain—
And love and love and love and Love. Amen.

December 28—Bless this day
Bless this year
Bless the wound-healing
O God, O God, Bless me. Amen.
Thank You.

December 29—*(Palm Springs)*
This is the archetype* down here: the Spirit's
upthrust around the open feminine. Healing and
finding possible. Healing the imperiled Substance
and finding meaning in my life ahead. I see more
meaning in my life below. But now what is wanted?

December 30—My spirit is happier this morning and
for that I am grateful. My spirit has to learn to live
with an impaired life.

---

* As defined by C.G. Jung, archetypes refer to universal psychic
   realities, repeatedly expressing themselves in human behavior. He
   speaks of them as "eternal presences."

December 31— Last day of 1986, a year I didn't live consciously enough. A year which lived me. Started and ended in sickness. There is a different way to live—now let me live it. Authority must come from Spirit-Substance.

J O U R N A L   1 9 8 7

January 1—Happy New Year—to affirm yesterday's vision of a real way of living—from blue bowl authentic with grounded authority. That is possible this year and must be worked with no matter what happens physically.

The Spirit must be willing to suffer for sake of Self—wherever the parent archetype constellated. I must try not to give in to it. To do the right thing for the wrong reason is to do wrong. Clearer on what it is to live from Self with balance and authority. There is great temptation to live from wrong place. Please God, Self is honest.

January 5—Home—to remember this day a year ago whan I entered hospital for two and half months.

Then Four Springs' summer of healing. Now I am alive—I bless life—and slowly will find out how to live. It has been a year of agony of Substance, of almost death. And now that I am alive, let there be Spirit out of Substance and healing for both this year.

January 8—Pneumonia—reason to be afraid. O
God of meaning. O God of life, why?

January 14—Time has gone unconscious. Now I
must take hold.

January 16—No pneumonia—there never was, and
I am given back life. O God, let me choose to live.

January 18—Soul—it must be honored. This way
does not help.

January 19—Yesterday, happy all day. Soul present.
God, I move with gratitude to be alive.

January 20—Stay with Soul, stay with God. Go
slowly. Welcome day in gladness. Enjoy cooking.

January 21—I mustn't be guilty because I make a
fuss, because I get upset, and don't just stay nice and
kind. Takes guts, just stay with love. Come, she-who-
almost-died and is alive—choose maturity.

January 26—Stay creative, enjoy God, trust flow.
Awake into energy—not too much. Thank God for
energy, juices, meaning in moments.

January 29—I learn how vulnerable I am.
Hold sober consciousness this day.

January 30—(To Sea Ranch*) May that which wants soul be satisfied. Enjoy life this day. Bring love this day. That is your gift. Joy—Humor. Be true.

January 31—It is beautiful here. Some peace— glad for yesterday's talk. I get too jumpy. Need to love more of this quiet being of myself.

February 2—Happy Birthday to Rob *(her son)*— may this decade be maturing—make you a man— deepening meaning and authority for you.

Last day at Sea Ranch—hold with this peace of containment. Yesterday played with waves and ran for first time since hospital.

February 3—Home—O, my Lady, come home with me. Pattern—Pattern. I said I didn't dread coming home, but I didn't remember how I longed to stay at Sea Ranch. Spaces—not closed in—air, light, vista, objective place, time for dialog, quiet relatedness. Please this day let tenderness prevail.

February 6—This day, step by step—please remember my soul, remember joy, and how to move quietly, relaxedly, with ritual. Stones from the ocean, what do you tell me?

February 9—God, I lost You yesterday, pledge to honor You. My soul, my reality, my identity. With

---

* Sea Ranch is located on the northern California coast, appreciated for its beauty and silence. We visited there often.

You, I tell the truth. Play piano today, honor these instruments you love.

February 10—I didn't play piano, but did remain objective.

February 11—Best analytic hour with Dr. B. Am now on macrobiotic diet and it helps.

February 13—*(Four Springs)* As I drove up yesterday, I realized to play the piano for joy is the thing. Joy for its own being. So it is not a matter of urgency, do this or that before I die—but of joy, now, do this or that.

February 14—Happy Valentine's Day.
Grateful to be alive and not in hospital.
Bless this day. May I stay with heart.

Little spider, I regret killing you.
Suddenly I felt awkward—
wish I could give you back to life.

February 15—Wrote pages during two and a half hours listening to Mahler, of how calamity comes unbidden. One's only choice to say "yes"—and at end of symphony felt flow of music met by flow from Other—that resurrection is suddenly given and we say "yes."
Bless this day.

February 15—(Dream) A man's voice in front of my head saying, "Joan."

February 15—Now home—stay with consciousness. Plan for joy. Let each step be joy. Look, blossoms are coming. Magnolias saying hope. Cherry in masses, and that white cloud. Is it these that brought life so long ago? These are resurrections.

February 16—I can say "I give thanks for being bitten." Yes I am changing—yet O Lord, O Lord, enough?

February 17—O thank You, that yesterday I bought the "Prophet Bird" by Schumann. Memories of childhood sitting by my teacher's piano.

Today, there will be rhododendrons and violets—these are all gifts of the moment.

February 19—And so be warned. Yesterday did get rhododendrons and violets—and returned later to find the rhododendron fallen over. I leaped from car to right it. Car rolled back into street. Everything all right, but what message? Stay with sensation in body—learn from car. Let nothing pull from center. I give thanks for warning.

February 22—Bought daffodils for garden and two more roses. How to go slowly enough? Bought

piano music of "Prophet Bird." Can I learn now
to play the piano?

A whole day of quiet: work, food, piano,
talking.

February 26—Feeling better. To stand in garden
yesterday and just look and feel that surge of joy,
an old nourishment of Soul I lost touch with!

February 28—This day may I have the energy to
open poems of R. It brings creative energy I touched
in past with him.

March 2—The symptoms continue. Why always
Monday morning? I did not stay relaxed yesterday.
I need to face the doctor. Where is truth, where—
where is truth? I am having struggles over
macrobiotics. The "relief of normalcy." For a month
I have been obedient. Seemed an absolute
necessity—but for years ahead? No. Now what? Am
I like the alcoholic—all or nothing?

March 4—O, how I long for a Savior—one unified
whole system which will make everything right and
healed. I realize I cannot all by myself follow
macrobiotics. What do I project?

(Dialog)

I: O Thou, my Savior within, which balances
         opposites.

Savior: I am here.

I: Please be really here and not in word only.

Savior: Call me into your cells.

I: But You have never stayed all day,
          or in moments of need.
          You have never gone on calling me.
          I want to learn to hear You within
          I know You are there.

Savior: I will come more this day.
          Thank you for wanting me.

I understand more about Savior than betrayer. Stay in touch with Savior within and with defilement within.

March 7—(Sea Ranch)

May this voyage be blessed. As I drove up, felt waves of presence learning to live moments of Savior within. Overall I feel so well. This day I will search and dialog.

(Dialog with Savior)

I: O Savior, why have You been so long?

Savior: Here always here and you not knowing
          Here always here and you not helping.

I: Please stay now.

Savior: It is our dance together. Alone I cannot.
          We can see world with wisdom.
          Yes, you express me in walking, doing, now.

(Dream) She is a small older woman who speaks to me and offers me something. I refuse. Then am intrigued and return. She gives me juice, paper on which she has

written something that looks interesting—short and
long lines scattered on the page. She leaves no name or
address. We are meeting tomorrow at 7:30, she says.
I say we are leaving and she says not before then.

(Dialog with a woman figure from dream.)

I (to woman): Who are you?

Woman: I could help you if you'd pay attention
to me.

I: How could you help?

Woman: By giving you the strength of your own
irrational. I am so lively and alive in you and
you're afraid of me and prefer to be passive.

I: It's not that I don't enjoy you but you are
archetypal and partial. You leave me
suddenly empty.

Woman: I don't say be possessed by me—
just relate to me.
Couldn't you enjoy me and still stay with
yourself?

I: No, I give you all my identity. You see,
you're substantial and I am not.

Woman: Can you learn to honor the identity of who
you are? You are beginning to enjoy your
sense of peace.

I: O.K. until I am hit by calamity of identity.

Woman: I will defend you.

I.   I guess I think you judge me.

Woman: But I don't. I admire you.

I: So I can be helped by irrational feminine.

March 9

(Dialog with God)

I: My Thou Beloved

Thou: I am here, my Joan blessed.

I: I am here.
          More here because of Thou,
          Now in Your presence.

Thou: Joan, stay with me. Yes, you want to talk to
          feminine and will but now stay with me. So
          rare, so rare are these hours together. I move
          to you now with the feminine.

I: O Thou, suddenly I feel what Life
          might be like and regret unlived years.

Thou: Even now, don't project me
          I am in—with you, not another.

I: But I am not alone.

Thou: You could be. I am yours.

I: O Thou Beloved. I do love You.

Thou: Thank you.

I: Thank You.

March 10 (Home)

(Dialog)

I: My Thou Beloved.

Thou: I am here.

I: I am here—stay with me here at home.

Thou: Go slowly. Don't be afraid.

I: There are too many possibilities. Until last
night I had not faced the terror that it might
come back. I'm not asking You, just stand
with me. Something in me says "it's not."
What shall I do? Help me not to be afraid. I
don't know what the heart-pounding sound
is I wake to. Why the bruises, the red spots?
Is something wrong?

March 11—God, have mercy
Christ, have mercy
Low platelets perhaps transfusion.
O Self, stay with me for steady healing.

Bless this day, Substance, Spirit.
Thou—Covenant—sky,
and go in mercy. I have leukemia
Joy Joy Joy Mystery. Why!
Now we must work together. Amen.

March 12—Today I go to the hospital. Woke with a
throbbing head. It is hard to know what I feel—pain,
anticipation of pain—another long journey. Will I
live? My own ultimate reality. God, what is Your Will
for me? Why is this needed?

Joan, when you get home again, when you sit again in this bed, be prepared to live very differently. More authenticity is still wanted. More truth. You must get in touch with that authority that wants Life.

O Feminine, I need You. I am prepared to suffer. Please stay with me.

I stay with all the tenderness and dignity of You.

O Self, I will help you Be in all ways.

O creative animus, we'll think clearly.

O God, I am bound by this Mystery.

O Joan, I am here to carry consciousness.

March 13—Facing much more infliction of return of leukemia.

This is a last day of clarity before more chemotherapy. I regret I didn't live this year with more clarity, be more active in what my footprints wanted. I don't need to finish my book. But to express Love, what matters in life. Image the future of generations—grand, great granddaughter, life that will go on.

Now—to be more living more facing of reality. I do want to live, please God. Go to my cells, fight for life. One wants to know the odds and then fight. Enjoy the beauty of this life—really look. Enjoy love of this life—really look. Enjoy the chances to be in this life, really Be. The Savior is *now*.

March 21—Shared with Dr. B. (my analyst, who visited me) the joy moments. I think he was stunned but then understood them as affirmation of Self that is finding completion. E. recognizes this as Self.

And Joy, Joy, Joy in upwellings of tears. No leukemia left in test. Helped, I believe, by my letting go and saying Yes to life. And dream last night of a Rainbow Covenant breaking and dissolving into a new form of Covenant. I give Thee thanks.

March 28—God wants relationship worked with and not run from. I need to be open to criticism and open to giving criticism. To live is much more challenging than to die—now—strength of choices—willingness to suffer and even cause suffering.

March 29—This day I pray for white healthy blood coming. The bone marrow feeling loved. Life feeling welcomed. Trust again the effort of life and I will work with you.

April 1—Feeling happy. Learning how to deal with itch in night. Strange how good life feels. Some people coming. E. comes everyday and helps my commitment.

    Amazing talks with people
    Blood, Blood, come today.
    Mature Joan wants to pray.
I give such thanks for healing energy.

April 10—Feeling better than I have for years. Clear-headed, clear energy, and authority. How horrible to have been so searching and tired and now I have been found.

April 13—The absolute and utter amazement
of this day. The platelets are coming. Halleluia.

One month in hospital.

I keep visualizing white cells coming.

I suddenly heard myself saying to my nurse,
"I have gone down into my cave and then heard
myself. And immediately the jeweled serpent has
come and brought me back out." I give thanks.
Bless this jeweled serpent.

What was I doing in not acknowledging that
leukemia might return!
"Others—yes—but not me!"

Somehow did I think I would be carried
by the angels?

April 14—I do see more clearly how death-rebirth
archetype has been constellated for me; my almost
dying at birth, my sister Barbie's tragic death at four,
my mastectomy, and now—But how do this, short
of the actuality of dying?

April 15—I told E. I suddenly understand there has
been something shining through me all these years
that others have responded to. But I was not with
ego connected to it. Now I am and I give thanks.

A great sadness that I have never really known
myself enough. O Substance, I will love you this day.

O Spirit, let's love Substance.

And a child may be, is being, born from this.

April 19—E. added yellow thread to resurrection
rainbow. God, bless most this amazing day.

April 21—I've been so afraid of death and now death is a beloved friend. How can this be!

April 27—This day I was supposed to go home, but I am here, sick, on oxygen, weak. Why? Not ready yet. Bless memories—let wholeness come. There are memories and thoughts. Who has Jesus been to me?

April 28—Still in hospital. I want to go home but need to stay here until well.

All these days, bless this slow healing process.

May 1—Today—bone-marrow biopsy and facing truth about leukemia. I don't feel I can go through another chemotherapy. May I do Thy Will. I remember from early days, "The Lord preserve you and keep you and the Lord make his face to shine upon you and grant you Peace." Amen.

May 3—Bone marrow no leukemia. So I go home. I give great thanks. Rainbow Covenant, stay.

May 4—Home. What a beautiful healing place!

Within the confines of this day

I pray, I pray, I pray, I pray

(Dialog)

I: My Thou Beloved.

Thou: I am here. My Joan blessed.

I: I am here. Bless this day, a day of conscious-
        ness. Thank you for yesterday's joy of white
        flowers against blue sky.

May 6—Bless consciousness—strength
Earth Mother, in kindness come
        For life has hard edges.
        I am startled at them.

May 15—To hospital with infected blood.

May 17—God, is it possible that what you want is in
the small things done, choices made, your concern is
not life and death, which are natural processes? Is
Your concern the supranatural choices within the
natural? I feel my serving of battles serves You. A
small choice—but a step for You. For You to save my
life, does that serve You? I can try to save my life, so I
can go on serving.

May 21 —Going home today. Better plan for Sea
Ranch, for not knowing when something else comes.
God, encompass me and my journey.

May 22—Is it true that God doesn't care whether I
live or die—but does care how I live or die? Bless this
home—
        O God, do care whether I live.
        God, grant me mercy.

June 4—Having laid awake facing the future. How do I live with the fear of death so close? I see more clearly what is meant by courage. I've been hiding, yielding secretly and see clearly today that I must choose life and stand with life with courage in every choice. And call a healing factor to be in my bone marrow, in my blood, in my soul. "There is that best." Let this be the first day of the rest of my life.

June 7—What shall I do for consciousness? Last night's dream was of a dream with mosaics and four icon-like figures and four crosses. I am using it to tell a group about symbols. I need, I know, to affirm pattern and order within me. And of bone marrow cells as they form the pattern and order of my blood cells. What needs to die now for rebirth? Some old father-rigidity must go. Let creativity flow in four directions. Poetry, art, music, humor. Let the unconscious be expressed. Let colors flow. It doesn't have to make sense to anyone. Higgeldy-piggeldy-flow. Let out the bubbling idiot. Honor her. Let her artforming have some place for the first time now.

June 11—I need a world view large enough to encompass all that is happening. I need to understand birth and death. The whole mystery of life, O Great God who encompasses all mystery, I ask You to help me rise in courage.

June 13—O God, as I pray for life, I remind You twice I've had leukemia, chemotherapy. My body cries out. I cannot take more. O, remember me. O

God, I don't want to die. What shall I do now? It is
not to do things. Not just to endure, or escape life,
but live.

June 15—After last night's dream, God's presence
personal. How else can God say, "Yes, I am with
you?" God, do You care about my life, that it
continues, not as existence but as meaning? After talk
yesterday with E. about wanting quality time, not
just existence, I know I mustn't split God. God,
encompass both possibilities with meaning in both. I
must see I am in a total process with God everywhere.

   "The order in your bowl encompasses your
death from leukemia." Ask leukemia, then, "What do
you serve?"

June 21—(Sea Ranch) This I don't believe—to be
again at this window—grasses, green cypresses, sea.
There is is my blue bowl. In the hospital, to have
wondered would I ever see this again—and now here
in actual flesh and blood. I give thanks. The bird
soars, the wind blows in grass.

   Yesterday I cried betrayal that leukemia came.
Now, in talking with E. I try to put this into a larger
context of meaning, which I have gained by being
forced up against the ultimate. I didn't really hear it
with mastectomy or first leukemia—but now I do, in
waves. I shudder. This is my life? Did this come to
force me to consciousness? I have not been able
earlier to grasp really the impact of some dreams. To
know God at work in them for my wholeness, to
know the psychoid possibility of healing. Please, God.

June 21—A dream says "endurance" is the answer. What does that say? It calls for patience. O You who bring this answer, stay with me and I will stay with You.

Can I have the honesty to work among all these parts of me? There is a Great Mother in me, help me to stay with healing. Pour out this healing process into the veins, arteries and bone marrow of me.

June 22—What do I want of my life? It says carry your own consciousness, know when you are vulnerable. I have no doubt of God's love—that fills me. The irrational must be included, as warned in last night's dream. It had felt like death to permit it—and death not to permit it.

June 23—Now this is Farewell to Sea Ranch. I think nothing prepares for the day of departure. It is an archetypal break and the grief is great. Two gold flowers in cave remind me. The standing stones are there. This morning's talk on choice helped. I don't believe it. After all those hospital days, it is still unbelievable to look from the broad window at leukemia—and now, Good-bye.

P O E M S :   J U N E   1 9 8 7 *

The River

Absolute delicacy
Held
between bold and silence
Within a rock, stream, tree, mountain
Forever and Now
See!

Ocean Meadow

Home
Bronze undulation
Horizon cup
Soul.

Solstice

Light forms shimmering
Around the globe enveloping
In light in light in light
Silently the darkening other strength to be ashore

* Written during her stay at Sea Ranch.

To stop the happening fingers of the light
Listen—the universe is still—waits
Then sighs as darkness starts to flow
Against the light.

Healing

Feel in deep recesses of substance
Call patterns come to balance
Balance dark and light inhale exhale
Heart beat and beat
Bone marrow, pulse now with good creation
Come—come—come
Life emerges! Come

Black Virgins

O my sisters, I bring you my body
Eternal dark feminine
Walk in compassion my veins
Deeper, deeper than all my thought
Walk with dark slow purpose
My life's meaning.

*   *   *

O God of midnight hours
Immeasurably close
Immeasurably far away
Confront my bone marrow with Your words of life
Sacred authority says Life Is
Life Is. Life is wanted
Wanted by the deepest furtherest surest sphere

of God
Life Is
Hear
And obey.

* * *

Grasses golden say, "We are always here,
        bending flowing with the wind."
Ocean calls to me, "I am always here."
Heart, heart are you there and here ?
Bring "there" here now.
Hold me in that love which is eternal.
As if this were all—all there ever was
This moment of being
Now held in the still of nature
Visible only leaves in gold and green
The purpose of the breeze, the birds intent
All else in stillness waits
And waits and waits
The slow pregnancy of change.

(JOURNAL RESUMES)

June 26—What will it take for me to recognize
evil—not just out there—but in here—in me and in
my immediate world? The family pattern of "see no
evil," somehow to stay separate, untouched. Anyone
who "rocked the boat" was evil. I've seen this in
many of my family.

I see both now in myself and my child.

I pray meaning of this illness

It is revealed in its healing.
Slowly Thou—I pray for meaning—
Understanding that I do Your Will,
thus bring depth and laughter.

June 27—I must be able to live and not run away.
You who make patterns, grant me strength and
consciousness. A dream of a midnight butterfly.

June 29—Home—God have mercy worked on in
night. Good news on bone marrow. I must affirm
the positive.

July 4—Worked all day on how I let destructive
thoughts poison me—an alternative to using my own
strength to deal with situations.
     I awoke convinced I must start with poetry—
so wrote two poems today.

July 4—*(Four Springs until end of August)* Dream
of pattern on ceiling that *Is*.
     Old image keeps rising of what I am—and I
cannot find who I am until I let go of the old image.

July 12—Journal thoughts have been expressed in
poetry. Just facts here.
     A robin—or a thrush. A doe running. Sound of
fox. Inward longing to move but muscles unwilling.

July 13—Place is prodigal with nature. Distant doe—
flash of tanager—race of baby foxes—high vulture.
Still. Still. Still. Think. There is this moment only.

What is happening? Island of peace around me. But
problems in seminar. How stay with healing flow and
include darkness? Don't split them. It is all one world.
I must focus on healing in all parts, not just in bone
marrow. God, who am I? Please be here in mercy.

July 14—Whatever strength I have is needed here.
Right here in the particularity of my life. To give
what I can give. What am I so afraid of in life? Why
can't I rise to free what must be freed. If I can face
death I can face life—whatever realities, choice, facts.
O God, rise in me. Be simply clear. There are things
that can be done. I must and can come back from
the limbo land of sickness. My head is clearer now.

July 15—O misery, misery. Do I need to see where
pain must be and at least make it purposeful?

July 17—There is necessity of the Will of God this
day—not consent to be unconscious. I want balance
between opposites—between fear and joy, strength
and weakness, vulnerability.

July 18—Yesterday decided to memorize the Tewa
prayer beginning, "What I am, I must become."
These words evoke the Self in me. I brought it to
bread and wine—as though the bread were what I
am, and constantly ingesting it helped the becoming.
Also related to "Be thou thyself and I shall be
thine,"* and "Before I formed you, I knew you." **

* Nicholas of Cusa, Christian mystic.
** Jeremiah.

July 19—From a dream I see need to stay with the objective animus. He sees and accepts facts. Realities simply are. With my bone marrow and immune system, let go, let go to healing. Work at healing.

O God, how together do we heal? I trust you want healing—want for me what can emerge as life. Relax to that which heals substance, and that which heals soul.

July 23—Yesterday bitten by a tick and so I'm on medicine. Why? What message? Synchronicity at banquet gave me "Joy of the Lord." Opposites. "Choose life," says God. I must be more active in my choice of life.

July 28—Last night confronted by fear which wants to be heard. Then dialoged with God Transcendent who talked to bone marrow and affirmed life. God Transcendent incarnated within me to help with back bone needed these days.

PRAYERS AND POEMS:
JULY 1987

Now I am here, Lord,
To live what is left of my life
O God, my substance hungers for Thee
O God, into this day come
O Virginal, be open to impossible new
O Spirit, come in your urgency for Substance
O Child, be manifest
Not I, but Thou who lives in me.
Amen.

* * *

God, Your hieroglyphic on the tree
Two baby foxes dangling from a branch
Askew of legs and tail—and gone—
A message of a moment
A great imprinter, present to our need
If I know You in foxes
Shall I not know You in marrow of my bone
Your hieroglyphic in my body stamped
In the moment! See
It is There.

* * *

Sunset gathers into passing time
The party's eternality
Blood—stirring tone, calm swirling
Eyes and feet released from daily
Love, you are present
Now in twilight silence
The deeper party dances on.

* * *

O moment that music
Enters every cell
Holy healing drop of sun and green
And music overpowered
Everywhere, all cells
All that is of Life, bathed
infused, transformed.

* * *

Word, out of stillness, come
Healing flow, come
Somewhere let anxiety dissolve
Hands, ease the pattern around me
Sand mandala, speak healing wisdom
Foxes come in free pattern
Deer flow in freedom
Quail from up the hillside
Cloud float
And I, obedient, come.

Star

At first the twilight sky was flat
As though a hand could smooth it.
Slowly then deeper as though one could see into
Always into—sameness—yet perhaps
Suddenly one star—found—gone—found
No more—one star
Eye of God peeping through obscurity
It watched us turn and walk away
And blessed us every step.

* * *

Bone Marrow

Mysterious core
Center of the mandala of the frame of me
So much depends on you
Soft creative center
Will of God in pattern
You, creator of pattern
You, center of pattern
Hold in obedience to depths that know
Pattern and chaos
And beyond them both the mastery
of pattern which is meaning
Pattern which serves the God of evolution
Come
To summon us
to Consciousness.

*August 5—(Dream) A letter from lawyer tells me
to take hold of destiny, responsibility, to love the
complexities, not as disaster, but as meaning. God
of meaning, come.*

August 8—(Dream) I carry a gold egg near my heart.

August 11—Out of the seminar such meaning.
The Weiman quote—the best in every situation.
Tillich—our neurosis as way of avoiding nonbeing
by avoiding being, and Nicholas of Cusa—"Be thou
thyself and I shall be thine." Deep sense that
commitment is the human side of Covenant, and
Pattterner is the Pattern.

   What in the love of myself shall I give myself?
The line between birth and death is incredibly
narrow. I still want life.

   O God in my bone marrow, heal and bring
Pattern.

August 13—This is 10th anniversary of my
mastectomy. I recommit myself to do the Will. It is
obedience to the best in every situation, outer and
inner. The inner best is not my neurosis. And the
outer best is not inertia. I meet the subtlety with
which the inner archetypal world invades the outer.
O God, I match Your Covenant with mine.

*August 13—(Dream) A man inserts crystal—jewel
sparkler in my feet to protect them.* (Like sparkles on
river yesterday.)

August 14—Not enough to want to do the Will—
or will to—I must do it with so strong a pledge that
it will be remembered—and see also not just in
situations but inwardly to do Thy Will.

August 15—The nature of God is forgiveness. So
Jesus knew in baptism as different from John the
Baptist's split of wrath and forgiveness.

August 17—Jesus—and God—what an amazing
man. Seminar—the best—forgiveness as
process—unity of opposites—unfathomable.
        What Jesus knew of God—wilderness to cross.

September 7—For so long I've had the experience of
poison in my mouth, in dreams. Now the saliva is for
a healing ritual, meaning I am no longer poison to
myself! O Bone Marrow, let healthy cells come
dancing up.
        Lady of the Lake
        Lord of beauty
        Come into my Substance
        For choiceful joyous living
        This day.

September 10—Feel from visit with doctor yesterday
her assumption the leukemia will return.

September 16—How shall I keep more related to
facts in my unconscious? Ego has often been gripped
when unconscious breaks through. But I hear here

ego needs to break through more to unconscious
and keep related to it.

September 17—Heard today from Dr. T. that I have
leukemia again. Have I always known this?
Shocked—numb. I will see her tomorrow about
what to do—think I will choose against
chemotherapy.
    O God of Mystery, why?
    O Bone Marrow, have I not loved you enough
    At banquet at Four Springs, I got the words,
"all inclusive"—"cup", and I said "yes" and here it is.

September 20—Went to child abuse conference,
as my last experience with psychological collective,
before I die. Out of it, a vision of my life—neurotic
beginning—emergence —strength—Peace.

THE PROCESS OF DYING: THE FULFILLMENT OF MY LIFE

September 22—What is symbol to me is not necessarily symbol to another. "You can't take it with you" applies also to symbolic meanings. "All these things you loved—whose shall they be?" I have to be willing to let their meaning die with me. I know I shall not see my new rhododendron bloom again, or smell my daphne ever. I wondered in the spring. Now I know what I can give to others—openness about death—talk of it with meaning. I asked my nurse why I had so much vitality now, while so tired all summer. She said, "Perhaps your change in attitude now you know you are dying." Yes, the Self is constellated with great energy, as I felt when I went to hospital in March. All summer I worked on visualization of life which was right to do.

September 24—So hard to say goodbye to Guild group last night.

I asked the nurse what lay ahead? Loss of energy, some secondary infection. At some point a choice to stop chemotherapy and tranfusions.

September 25—I was known by God before I was born—so nothing that happens is a surprise, as even this dying is now a pattern, so can't speak of "cause"—no "if onlys"!

September 26—A sense of accepting myself crying—more emotion than I have had.

September 28—The words in my head, "my life is a song." Today—absolutely happy—absolutely nothing to dread or worry about. Isn't that amazing—with death ahead?

September 30—I do not have to "judge for myself what is right"—part of my reality is to accept that I have always projected authority. That's no disaster—is meaning.

Today decided not to go to hospital for antibiotics that could prolong but leave me to die in hospital. I chose quality time at home. Martha T. *(the doctor)* came and was loving and spoke of my courage.

October 8—I do wonder that in the past I so feared death. I don't fear death now. The mystery, unknown, meaning, fulfillment of my life. Gratitude to be given opportunity for fulfillment and meaning. Pray for kind and quiet death, when time comes.

October 9—In answer to a question whether my body was making ready for death as it would for childbirth, I said no, that childbirth was natural and my death is not a natural one as in old age, but an unnatural killing of myself by leukemia. Therefore I expect resistance to death by the rest of my body, which doesn't want to die. Yet death as a process must be known by my flesh.

It is still hard really to "know" I am dying, for I feel so well.

I wonder—what is the moment of death—do I just "go out"like a light—is there some consciousness remaining?

I am so clear about my substance and I plan my services, think of cremation where the "fire and the rose will be one," think of my ashes at Four Springs, plan for familiar rocks, greens, wood to go on my grave—all that is very real—and the future for other people, who they are becoming. But me—this essence—this consciousness of me—the more it is increasing in the dying process, the sadder I am that it must end.

October 11—The hospice nurse tells me dying will be a slow process—not of infection, but after each transfusion, not back quite as far as before—and then a time when transfusion will no longer help and final problem from lack of red blood or platelets. My body shudders.

October 12—I do see that it is the archetype of death that constellates possibility for people. They are

willing to take long, impossible strides in its presence
that hitherto seemed out of the question. I see things
happening to members of my family, new
possibilities. I am awed.

October 16—It is so hard to stay conscious while
dying. Body is distressed. When I get a transfusion,
as today, I am both keyed up and separate from my
body. Now I need to learn this happens and prepare
for it.

O God, I have been giving thanks for being
granted a conscious death. Then I must not fail to be
conscious. It is such a temptation to give in to body
unease and go blotto. I am clearer now on the
"work" required of me in these closing days.
Somehow I do not "know" enough that I am dying.
Am I just cut off from my feelings, and so seem
courageous to others? It is so hard to feel myself still
enacting old neurotic patterns. Dying should be a
triumph of the Self—and I see now I may die in
pettiness. Why don't I "judge" for myself what is
right? I fail God in not being clear with my authority.
Now—let me carry it—authority, consciousness,
relatedness and Love. Let this be the first moment of
the rest of my life. I call on you, God, to help me. O,
Holy Spirit, if these are the last hours of my life, I
need You—and thank You.

October 20—After trying to prepare my son to face
and be ready for being overcome by grief at my
death—at that instant between the "isness" of a
person and the "not-isness" of a person—I now see I

must also prepare for myself—grieve now for myself,
no time later. Or trying to be heroic—but in
moment of facing death I face that abyss. Grieve
now—grieve now for all that is left behind—so in
that moment I can say *yes* with courage.

Die to become—all that must die in me before
I am able to die—all attachments, all control. I'm
still attached to life, to my own body.

October 22—Having touched the edge of death two
days ago, I'm now living resurrected life—each day a
jewel. After transfusion, breathing better.

So hard to know I'm dying. Realized in
moment of crisis, I'm not ready. I don't want to die.
What shall I do? I now understand yearning for a
miracle—that the impossible yet come to pass.

I am in awe of the act of death as different from
the process. I've felt content to be in the process as
long as the actual moment be down the road. But if
the actual moment is here, horror grips me. I don't
want to go through that moment. Not believing in
anything after death is hard, leaving me facing being
just extinguished. And while I would like to think
something happens to the achievement of
consciousness, nobody down all the centuries has
ever come back. Yet why does the conviction persist?

I am now dialoging in addition to "My Thou
Beloved"—to "God Transcendent," which is very
helpful and challenging.*

---

* The dialogs and prayers had been more with the Immanent aspect of
  God and now included the Transcendent.

October 24—(4:30 a.m.)—O God, what is the meaning of life? What is Your intent in creation? What do You want achieved by the end of time? Or is there an end? Does it all go on forever and why—to what purpose? What would You want of me? Why am I dying now? Is this Your purpose or Your mistake, or do You know or care anything about it all? I have to believe You care. I have to believe my life and death have some meaning in the totality of things. I want to believe my consciousness achieved goes somewhere after I die. Does it? Does it matter to You that I am trying to be whole? I must believe it does. What do You want of me before I die? How long—hours, days, months, years—How long? I say I have let go, but I am fascinated by life, its beauty, its paradoxes and people—the depth possible between us—You and I and our increasing intimacy. I want to go on living. Forever? No, but to a more natural fulfillment. O God Transcendent, what do You want of me? "Just Be," God says, "be who you are, be true, authentic and unafraid. Help one sector of life be real." And I answer: "And why am I dying?" And God answering, "Are you—or aren't you truly living for the first time? Be glad that you are truly living. The conditions are not the issue. Live." "Thank You," say I, assuaged.

October 28—This I of I which is conscious of being me—I believe this goes on in some form. All that a lifetime has achieved of consciousness can't just vanish—poof—at death. Do I go on to God? to add

to the consciousness of the great Transcendent?
—something like that?

As of last night's writing, a sense of beginning
to "cross over" with my body—still a fever—
here—but something of me there with God. Taping
the "once upon a time" helped the sense of God
presence.

How lovely that the magnolia has some
farewell blossoms for me.

October 30—Having been off and on all night, life is
losing its quality living.

October 31—And yet there is fulfillment still to be
achieved and that is "quality."

November 1—Remember the story F.S. told of the
man holding out one hand, and God said, "Give me
both hands."

Yes—God—both hands.

November 3—Pain—dizzy—temperature up
—Yes—God—Both hands.

End of writing

*November 12—After a difficult night of struggle with
"yes-no," her last conscious sentence to me that morning
was "Everything will be all right." She had won the
greater Yes over the "yes-no."*

*On the morning of November 13, 1987, Joan
was surrounded by four friends and Psalms were being
read to her. Shortly thereafter, quite suddenly and
quietly, her breathing changed and she died. The
journey here ended.*

*Three dreams follow which perhaps best convey
what that journey had been.*

THREE DREAMS

Early in Analysis

I was coming up out of the water in a very small submarine. When I reached the surface, I cried out:
"O, my Lord, I bow my head.
It is Your Will that I hear the cry.
It is Your Will that I see the Child."

* * *

God speaks to man and says:
"My son, do not fade from my Presence.
Do not fall."
The man answers:
"Hold me."

* * *

Towards the end of her life

I am at home in a V-shaped house. The sun is setting and casting its light through the V-shaped house, illuminating the landscape in front of me, which is ocean, hills and trees. I sit between the setting sun and its reflection on earth and water, all contained in the sign of Victory.

On a November day twelve years earlier she had
written the following lines, her own Answer to Job.*
Like Job, she confronted the opposites in God, and did so
with her words and her living in the ensuing years.
Finally by 1987 she showed us all how firmly her
courage not to run from God had held.

Answer to Job

God speaks:

Shall I create good and not evil?

Shall I not will evil?

Shall I not will to destroy, utterly?

Shall I not invite the dying and death?

Shall I not violate all dreams?

Shall I not wreck all progress?

Shall I not abort transformation?

Shall I not destroy this earth?

Shall I not seduce your soul?

Shall I not utterly infect your relationship?

* See Vol. XI of the *Collected Works,* C.G. Jung.

Shall I not plant doubt in your heart?
Shall I not cause her to despair?
Shall I not ruin all dreams?

I: No, I choose against Your power
—   Puny human, I mock you
I: Yes I stand with love
—   Puny human I mock love
I: There are two of us
—   I am I
I: You are only part of God
—   You have never acknowledged me at all
I: Evil, power, strength, demander, whipper
—   You have suffered me within
         But chosen not to see me outside
I: I must acknowledge You
         I must never run from You again
         Never.

                              —November, 1975

                    F I N I S

THE EARLY YEARS
1984-1985

Two years before the onset of her illness in 1986, her journals showed how intent she was to stay loyal to her dialog with God and what was demanded of her by it. Excerpts from those journals for 1984 and 1985 are included here to give additional glimpses into the religious nature of her journey. What she struggled with interiorly as the leukemia progressed was already in progress prior to 1986. The entries which follow illustrate abundantly how fervently she sought to know and be known, to serve and be served by her God.

EXCERPTS FROM JOURNAL, 1984

(Approaching her 60th birthday)

What is different? Trust know something. Something
pledged—happened in archetypes. Yes, I am different
at 60—more conscious. More eyes open and open
mouth, open to speak gratitude gratitude gratitude
gratitude.

This day I pray consciousness
60 still is achievement.
May help come in me
that I may help outwardly.

Terror wracks my soul
So great it is, so utter
Beating upon the shores of myself

Battering, so I may know how
I live this day.
At last opposite: hope
Hope for all working out
Hope grant peace to my soul.

O, Mystery I awe your process
I emerge slowly from despair,
Can lift my head, smile, plan
and stay in awe of the "I know not what."

I am Joan—I am Joan
You who have lost me
You whom I have lost
Find, me, O please let me be found.

O Love, O feminine Goddess,
Hello. You are—
And I am Joan—
Together this day—Halleluiah.
O God, whom I feel not present
Suddenly in voice you come
Please stay, please grace this day
That meaning may be.

All right—quiet—what are you
that I so adore here at Four Springs?
Humor, meaning, creativity, Total Being.
To Be with all is to Love God with all
And feel beloved daughter in return.

O God, what is it to pray to You
Out of this seminar, Your opposites
And mine?
Really to see You needing consciousness from me
And I assuming evil in the nature of creation.
This is the cry I bring to You,
Because of what is achieved out of transformation.

Nothing natural is as beautiful
As is to You there is meaning in agony
In what can come from agony.
You have it all inside You
May it be my will to know Your horror.

Thank you, I do understand more of transformation.
That I am pulled by both—natural and
transformation—
And I pour into both,
But my creative end is transformation.
John the Baptist is great
But my kingdom requires transformation,
That I knew at baptism.
There is another birth.

More consciousness comes like pain.
Seeing has balance.
O God this lifetime let me see
For Thee and me.

Kingdom of God within me
Possible impossible reality
God come
God Be.

Can I look at all nature's loveliness
and think Hiroshima?
Think last night's dream of man with knife?
O Greater Love, Come.
Last night to the stars
"Do you know I am here

Do I matter to you?"
And an answer sense of "Yes."

What have I learned these days?
That darkness wants to be transformed,
That there is a best emergent everywhere,
That evil is part of God. (Still shocks me to put it
down. So as not to be surprised at reality again.
Reality not to be surprised.)

Fool, come,
Defend me.
You are the one I must defend,
O Fool, authentic Fool, beloved.

Somewhere Fool is separate from
This nervous judgment.
Fool has its own authority,
Serves God.

You who are Fool,
Only you can deal with evil,
Only you know how to dance.
All else is judgment and damning.
"Resist not" is your dance
And I know you need my honoring
As I need you, now.

Thou, without Your help in consciousness
Nothing can be done.
Ego's freedom is only a moment's liberty
Without the deep alliance of Your face.
I give thanks for Thee.

O God O God, as never before
Come, burn in me and in the beyond.
This place symbolizes human focus on God
and God concentrated, God so in essence,
God more available, everywhere present
Impinging, pressing, urging, wanting
Visible, flowing Not just fact, but known.*

God God
Felt come
Bless transformation—
It is not just God
But the power of God I call
I fear the name without the power.
Going home I pledge to call and call
And the power of God will come.

Monks living supranaturally
Four Springs lovely
Meditation room with bread and wine
All are mystery, be blessed.

November 1—(Approaching birthday)
O Sagittarius fire—Zeus—Jupiter,
Let me live from your authority, Venus—Taurus—
Help me this day.
God is my only home
Like Son of Man who has not where to lay his head
Nowhere, not even Four Springs can
replace God-home I carry in my heart.

* Written while at monastery, "Christ in the Desert," Abiqui, New
  Mexico, for a week.

Great Black Virgin of Einsiedeln
Black flesh, Black blessing
O God, O God, O God
Who am I?

Be yourself, O God help me to Be.
May I be the one you knew
Before You formed me.
To this is Birthday present, God.

(Night before birthday)—Do I die tonight?
What is the ending of the 50's?
I am afraid as if too big is planned
Remember me, remember this one struggling to live
Celebrate reality and potential
Toward the rest of my life. Toward the rest
of my life.

Who am I? O Joan, Joan
Who can tell you unless you know you are full
of being.
Claim essence,
Vulnerable, playful deep.
O Holy Face, tell me I am.

Pray courage, pray ability to die, to suffer.
What are you afraid of? Stop holding on—
Serve life, serve growth, serve God in evolution.
You almost died at birth
And lived to die by choice.

EXCERPTS
FROM JOURNAL, 1985

O God, I am afraid of Your darkness
Of Your whirling light I am afraid
Of the heart that breaks in the darkness
Of the moment shattered before born
I walk alone and not alone
From tomorrow yesterday appeals
In Thee there is friend and destroyer
Who am I and where shall we go?

Thank You for return of energy. That is rebirth?
What died? Fear of death. Fear of suffering, of agony.

Courage, Courage, Courage. Will, fired by Your
purpose. Goodbye to decade of growth and change.
God, will You please choose to use me for Your Will?
        Event in soul has come, now life,
now incarnation come.
O Thou, may I hear Your dreams in me.
Warning they are—disaster—
O Thou, how did Jesus know You within?
O Thou, how do I know You within?

Feminine, walk with me this day
O Feminine, come.
Steady God, steady in my heart
Go slowly day by day, serve the Will,
Serve gentleness and joy, serve Love.

Thou, may this day hold Your Will
May it be feminine—
I lose substance in exhaustion.
O Thou, have mercy on me.

O Word, why aren't You mine?
O Being eternal lived from core
Into my thought, my pen
Come incarnate, come.

Far beyond my death, Rob and Sharon,
        Records, writing.
Far between now and my death, love,
        laughter, God.

Slower day I pray
God of truth be with me
Authority taught by Jesus
Live in me that I be I.

Bless day, consciousness
that now which never was before

How can now consciousness come
Now born as never born before
Now, O why not now!

Is it consciousness gives form
to the pure imprint of creation?

Help with Being
It is not doing that is asked of me—
but Being. O God of I Am, help me Be.

Bless my religious heritage
Archetypal roots in me
To Jesus—my roots, my roots
Go back to You, my Lord.

Consciousness has to serve something.
Else it is bitter
O Love, O Third Point come
O Holy Spirit descend
That what is seen may serve Thee.

Conflict and authority:
"Let them light
And find you not a mouse."
Yes, some mystery is there
for me to walk this day.

O ache of soul, O consciousness
Where is God's joy that
I may enter in?

Go on, creative one,
Take it yourself
Take authority, judgment, choice
Carry the burden and the joy of God.

(Einsiedeln, Switzerland)
At Maria's feet I prayed healing of authority.
Heading down down down
into the dungeons of my heart
where blocks. Maria, heal, heal,
where I cannot reach.

(Zurich)
Bless this last visit to my analyst.
Bring truth for healing.
O soul, what do you want?
Bring truth for healing.

Bells claim Sabbath, Pentecost
Whit Sunday. O Bells, O Holy Spirit
Come bless consciousness this day.
To Become the who
Intended in the pattern
        of my Self—Yes.

(Jerusalem)
Bless Mystery known and unknown
Bless Thou present
O Blue flower in my heart
Blossom, encompass all.

O God, grant me energy
To bring healing and forgiveness
O God, grant me humility and wisdom
To move myself in healing and forgiveness.

O God, let me not forget You
The deep webbing of You
The deep presence of You
The deep ultimate terror of You
O God, I need Your help.

O God, I am afraid
I reach for You, cry for You
Be tangible Presence now.
O Thou, who will not let me go.

O day be blessed
Last day of seminar
First day of life to come
Authority Joy Being Love
Now Be Do.

Now Four Springs, welcome me
Time, Love, Consciousness
Present God stirs symbols alive
Fact alive within my ground.

Forgotten time
        O God Forgotten God
Presence now
        Be with me.

I feel energy—
O Thank you, God, for this life.
It is not what happens
But what I do with what happens that matters.
More energy. Last day of Seminar.

Really honored in toast at banquet. Lovely ritual.
Let this be day of consciousness
Let me know tree of knowledge of good and evil
Creating judgment, guilt and forgiveness.

Creative Judge, I don't know
        how to find you.
Creative Process of Life, come.

I am not Savior
Know, know
Blue flower is beside me
Savior within me.

Maria, have mercy
Forgiveness as Third Point I walk
To Your Will, I will
Your kingdom I serve.

The eye sees almost more than I can bear
And yet I must see more than I can bear.

O God, I yet must see
And do not see, O God please bless this day
Bless consciousness—Bless my eye of perception—
Bless my Self.

O eye of consciousness
this day comes. I want to see
Everything I want to see I can choose.
O God, help me choose.
This day O God of consciousenss

How will you come?
Thou unutterable Other
Evoked by Majesty in these tall trees
In this presence let me really see.

Soul, dance
There is still time to be
Soul have hope
Life before death can be
Soul come
This is the transformation wanted
Now soul now soul—BE.

Feminine who has come with voice and tears,
I pledge to stay with you
Remember yourself in my face
Remember yourself in my voice
You have remembered yourself in my tears
Remember yourself in my choices
Remember yourself in my love
I give thanks for return to being.

Queen Mystery, Grace
You Thou longing to return from exile
We wander and our time is now
It is still lonely in consciousness
Yet together we are not as alone
May your yearning be heard into my action
O in sisterhood is Mystery
This is forgiveness.

SOME RECORDED MEMORIES...

*There follow selected excerpts from one of Joan's tapes,
made April, 1987 while in the hospital*

Once after a Four Springs seminar that had to
do with Stations of the Cross, a friend told me of a
Carmelite chapel where there were interesting
Stations of the Cross. So I found the way, and I went
there, and I walked in through the gate and down
the walled roadway, feeling awe at these enclosed
women. Serving, serving people. And I tried to get
into the chapel, and it was locked. And so I went to
the door, another door there, which said, "Please
ring the bell at the turn." I thought "turn" was a
verb, and so I went inside and turned, and saw no
bell. Actually it's a noun referring to a curved inset in
the wall that turns on a turntable. And there is a
doorbell beside it. But I felt kind of lost there; I felt
like the traveller in Walter de La Mare's poem "The
Listener," saying to the void, "Tell them I came, and
that no one answered. That I kept my word." In that
stillness I looked around and saw a pad of paper and

a pen on a small table. I think at that moment I began to feel more like Alice in Wonderland. Was a little Box going to appear, and something say, "Eat me!"? So I went and wrote a note on that pad, "To Someone," explaining why I'd come and my present predicament, and left it there on the table, and walked away, past the silent wall and through the silent gate. Great numinosity, great numinosity. And a day or so later came an apologetic letter. The chapel was locked to keep the neighbors' children out, and if I'd just come again and ring the bell by the turn (and it explained what the turn was), they would give me a key, so I could always come, as often as I wished. I was amazed and delighted, as though God had answered in detail. And so I returned a-trembling and rang the little bell, and heard feet shuffling approaching; and a voice, "What may I do for you?" coming through the wall. I explained and was welcomed warmly; and the turn turned, and there was the key. And once I got into the chapel, more important to me than the Stations of the Cross was a stained-glass window, of Jesus knocking at a door. A strange enigmatic expression, but I've always gone back, and looked and looked. They said it was a copy of some card, or some picture in a book, but I've never seen the original. I returned many times; I met the Extern who wore earphones and listened to basketball games. Once to my horror, the garbage truck arrived just as I did. Somehow I didn't expect them to need such monstrosities as garbage trucks. I was encouraged to come to the morning masses at seven, and Sundays to a closure at four. I wasn't allowed to

take communion, but they gave me a missal book
with markings to follow, and a book by St. John of
the Cross. And we corresponded with each other
back and forth. And they said so few understood that
for them to pray was a work, and they seemed to be
glad for my understanding. It was that time that
Ruth Warnick was dying, and I asked their prayers for
her. And last year Elizabeth wrote to them of my leukemia and asked their prayers, and they responded.
And when I was better we went there and I thanked
them, through the turn.

What did they stand for? O, the numinosity of
those 7 a.m. masses, when that which was closed
between the two chapels was opened and one could
see into the other world, lit by sunrise, and the dark
figures of the nuns coming to the grill, one by one.
The Self, something dedicated to the religious value,
was deeply stirred in me by that.

* * *

I was terribly glad to find the man Jesus at the
Records seminar. This was a great relief to me,
although I had a hard time bringing the man
together with his relationship to the savior archetype.
I think I still do. Such thinking really stretches me.
And yet I did awaken one morning with a flood of
understanding about his relationship to the
Messianic, to the Virgin Birth, to Death/Rebirth, to
Wound/Healing, and was very moved that Elizabeth
picked up on this, and did a lot with it. I've always

adored leading *Records;* the numinous mystery of this
man's relationship to God so grips me. And so comes
alive when I lead the *Records.* And his openness and
wisdom. And his asking, "Why do you not of yourself judge what is right?" I've gone on feeling
addressed by that question, and I still don't think
I've ever really answered it.

When I went to Four Springs for the first time,
it was openness to truth that most impressed
me...And I think the presence of God must have
moved me greatly in the numinosity of ritual. Also,
the Lord's Prayer, rewritten in my own words, most
moved me; and I continued with it. It took my
second intermediate *Records* study before I began to
be deeply gripped by Jesus—his courage, his choices
—and I went out and wept after the passages on the
crucifixion.

Later, after participating in seminars, I entered a
training to lead them. Slowly, slowly, slowly I got at
home leading. I remember wonderful training
sessions, with the emphasis on leading from the
inferior function. I remember being on my knees
before the orb (in the Meditation Room at Four
Springs). Just before going in to lead: "Could I do
it?"...Sheila Moon once took me to Hoodoo Creek,
and had me choose a stone to push my hand against
while I led. I learned to look at each person as they
entered; and to keep each as a friend and not project
the collective "they." And to be conversational in my
leading, and to lead as though to one person. I
learned to be human in the leaders' chair, and to
bring humor. And to get up at four in the morning,

to be addressed by the material before I led it. And I gathered notebooks for the future on all passages, and all seminar activities. And still I say there's nothing like the Basic *Records* study.

* * *

I would like to speak of the Benedictine Monastery in New Mexico called "Christ in the Desert," near Santa Fe. What is there about the place? The almost undriveable long road in, with just a sort of vague note on the roadway that you are in the right place? Arriving, finally, and finding our names, Elizabeth and mine, on two cell-like rooms. No one to greet us. Walking to the chapel. It says something about, "Visitors, ring the bell." We rang the bell, still no one came. Finally, wandering into their meeting room and being welcomed, and taken to the kitchen to get our food. And those tiny cells with their wood stoves that we learned how to light, and the kerosene lamps. And the silences, and the high cliffs around, and the coyotes howling. And following our flashlights to the morning services; and those hooded figures around the room behind their kerosene lamps. And trying to figure out which book we were following. And the warmth of their chants, the guitar playing, the gentle loveliness of that music. And later the same: the guitar playing, the kerosene lamps, and their chants in the chapel. Wandering to the river. Going into depths in the haystack; two kinds of depths. And sharing in the guest living room, a hallowed place.

It is to say that "Christ in the Desert" was simply a hallowed place; it was filled with numinosity and my dreams spoke of it night after night, showing that my unconscious was just stirred by it. Again it touched that place in me of dedication to the service of God. And I long to go back there again. I've gone on corresponding with them; they also have prayed for me while I've been here in the hospital.

I do want to add that the last time I came home remembering some of the tunes that went with the chants. And at least one which went with a blessing, which was:

> The Lord bless you and keep you
> The Lord make His face to shine upon you
> and grant you peace.

Every time I sing that, or chant it, I feel the presence of "Christ in the Desert."

And then also was the memory of that canticle that ends,

> "O bless the Lord."